What Was It Like to Be a Knight?

By Carol M. Elliott

Scott Foresman
is an imprint of

Glenview, Illinois • Boston, Massachusetts • Chandler, Arizona •
Hoboken, New Jersey

Photographs

Every effort has been made to secure permission and provide appropriate credit for photographic material. The publisher deeply regrets any omission and pledges to correct errors called to its attention in subsequent editions.

Unless otherwise acknowledged, all photographs are the property of Pearson Education, Inc.

Photo locators denoted as follows: Top (T), Center (C), Bottom (B), Left (L), Right (R), Background (Bkgd)

ISBN 13: 978-0-328-47297-0
ISBN 10:   0-328-47297-2

5 6 7 8 9 10 V010 18 17 16 15 14

Table of Contents

Being a Knight

In **legends**, knights were brave heroes who battled evil. They protected women and the weak. They lived by a code of honor.

In reality, knights were strong, well-trained soldiers. They often worked for a **lord** who owned a castle and the land around it. Most knights went into battle when their lord called them.

Not just anyone could become a knight. Knights came from **noble** families. Noble families had money and important friends, such as a lord or the king.

Knights had to have money because they had to pay for their **armor**, horses, and weapons. These were expensive.

Becoming a Knight

A boy started training to become a knight when he was about seven years old. First, he became a page. A page learned about weapons, horses, and armor.

When he was about fourteen years old, the page became a squire. A squire worked for a knight. He served the knight and went to battle with him.

A squire became a knight when he proved himself ready. Between the ages of eighteen and twenty-one, a squire who had served well was dubbed a knight. This means he was tapped on each shoulder with a sword.

The Armor

A knight wore a coat of **mail** that was made of thousands of small metal rings. It had to bend easily so the knight could ride and fight. Plates of armor were worn over the mail.

A coat of mail weighed about 30 pounds.

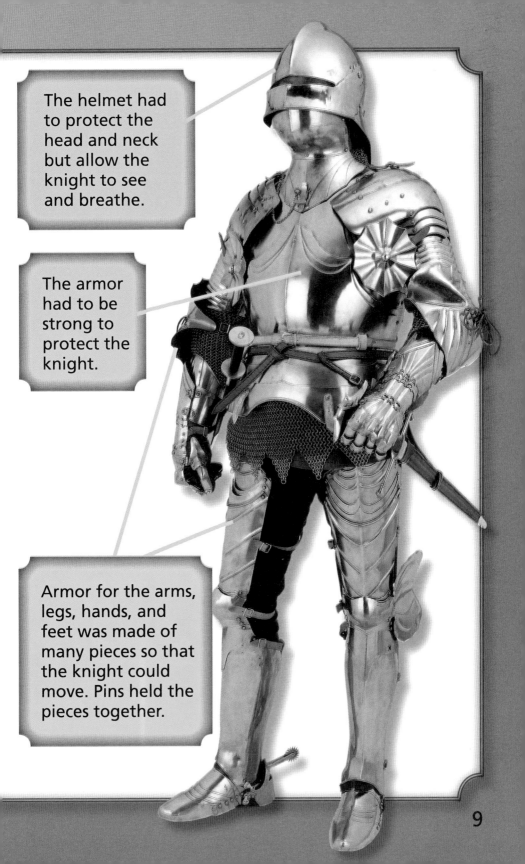

The helmet had to protect the head and neck but allow the knight to see and breathe.

The armor had to be strong to protect the knight.

Armor for the arms, legs, hands, and feet was made of many pieces so that the knight could move. Pins held the pieces together.

9

The Weapons

A knight carried a **lance**, which was like a long spear. In contests called jousts, two knights rode toward each other. Each would try to knock the other off his horse with the lance. In battle, many knights rode together. They charged the enemy with their lances.

Two knights charge each other in a joust.

If a knight's lance broke, then he had to fight with his sword. It could cut through mail and break bones, but it was so heavy that a knight had to use two hands to swing it.

The Quest

In legends, a knight rode off on his horse to fight giants and dragons, or he went to rescue a fair lady from an enemy. His trip was called a **quest**, and he had many adventures along the way.

In reality, most knights were too busy to go on quests. Knights managed the land around a castle and the **peasants** who lived on the land.

Peasants farmed the land, but the knight decided when to plant and harvest. The knight was a hunter and a rancher too.

The knight was also a judge when the peasants had fights and disagreements.

The Foes

In legends, knights fought their **foes**–evil creatures and dark knights who had turned from good to evil.

In reality, most battles were fought over land. Knights had to fight battles when their lord called on them to do so. Knights were brave, and they had to be. They could easily be killed or badly hurt in battle.

War changed when guns and cannons came along. Armor and swords could not protect a knight from these weapons. The days of the knight were over. But the stories of their brave lives still inspire us.

Glossary

armor *n.* a metal covering worn to protect the body in fighting

foe *n.* an enemy

lance *n.* a long, wooden spear with a sharp, metal point

legend *n.* a story from the past that is believed by many people

lords *n.* owners of land and of the people who live on it

mail *n.* armor made of metal rings

nobles *n.* people who belong to the nobility; persons of high rank or title

peasants *n.* poor farmers who farmed the land owned by the lords

quest *n.* a search for something

Reader Response

1. How were real knights like the knights in legends? How were they different?

2. Why are stories and movies still made about knights?

3. Would you want to be a knight? Why or why not?

Social Stud

Concept Literacy
Leveled Reader

Genre	Concept
Nonfiction	Exploring Cultures

Scott Foresman Reading Street 6.6.1

Scott Foresman
is an imprint of

PEARSON

ISBN-13: 978-0-328-47297-0
ISBN-10:   0-328-47297-2

9 780328 472970

90000>

Fannie Lou Hamer

Fighting for the Rights of Others

rweck Rice

TCM | Teacher Created Materials